Solitude's Embrace

Anna Belmonte

Inkfeathers Publishing
www.inkfeathers.com

Published by Inkfeathers Pvt. Ltd.
84, Janta Flats, Vivek Vihar,
New Delhi 110095, Delhi, India

Solitude's Embrace
Written by Anna Belmonte
Paperback Edition

First Published by Inkfeathers Publishing 2022

All Illustrations in this book are designed by
Greta Spitczok Von Brisinski

ISBN 9789390882632

www.inkfeathers.com

To the optimistic exceptions in my life - thank you.

Contents

Wishful

There are only two kinds
of people in the world,
Those that love themselves
and
Those that need a little help.

The feeling of
inadequacy
is perhaps the heaviest,
most unnecessary
burden borne.

It is too easy
to be led astray
by silver tongued lies
Than to trust mediocre
yet genuine truths.

The greatest
self-destruction
is embracing desolation
Over uneasy
yet forward momentum.

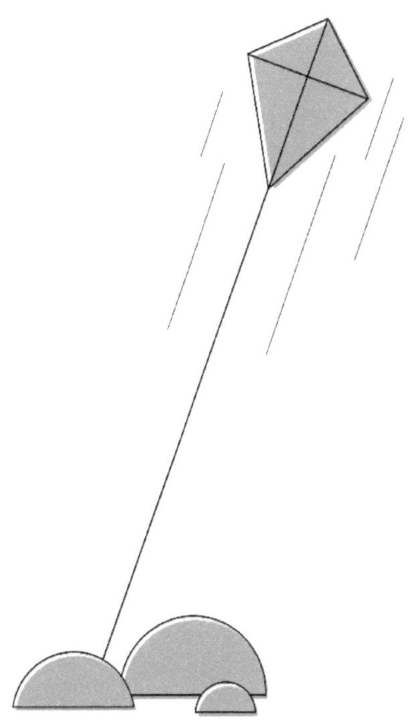

A soaring kite
is always safer tethered,
Grounded, guided
Rather than recklessly
blowing in the wind.

Quantify success,
Define the milestone
If not, life is wasted
chasing after a mirage,
shifting farther into
the distance
As time ticks by.

If everyone yearned
for centre stage,
Nobody would be left
to raise the curtain.
Allow them their individuality
For that diversity
permits harmony.

8

Strength is living well
without exploiting another's weakness.

Hold on,
For that which
aggravates
Will eventually
dissipate.

Wisdom is knowing how precious time is
before the minutes steal it away.

Let not today
yearn for yesterdays
But work for tomorrows.

Going with the flow
is a relaxed way of life.
Till reaching
the cliff of bad decisions,
going down
the waterfall of regret.

One is better off
following their own individuality
rather than anyone else's.

Tact
is superior
to destructive impulses.
Sensitivity
more valuable
than misguided honesty.

Though things weren't perfect,
she didn't despair.
It happened many a time, mimicked a pattern.
With its lows and its highs.
She had hope in her heart,
perseverance in her manner.
Every sunset promised a sunrise.

And the horizon promised her a better life.

She used rock bottom
to fuel creativity
Until a higher stratosphere
influenced positivity.

It would be humane
for the multitudes
to remember
that the adage goes
Climb the career ladder
Instead of the commonly practiced
Stepping on each other.

The amount of pressure
is the difference between
diamond,
flaunting their substance
and dust,
blowing with the wind.

A heart's beat is the sound of life.
And breathing plays the instrument.
Why walk out on this concert,
And risk missing
a show-stopping crescendo.

While beneath it,
sadness weighs so heavy
it skews one's outlook
But then,
maybe soon, maybe not
But eventually,
the breeze of euphoria
rolls through
sweeping it away like sand,
making room
for a lungful of relief.

Though one's path
seems long,
Taking the easier route
proves futile in the end
As the key to handling
the destination
Lies in the lessons
along the way.

Arbitrary capitalisation
is frowned upon;
In language,
by academics.
Otherwise,
by those that don't benefit.

Countries separated by boundary,
wars created by greed, even anarchy.

They fight for oil, they fight for territory.
But not enough for humanity.

Families left broken, with senseless carnage.
Lands left barren, with collateral damage.

The lessons taught to little children,
Must be relearnt by grown women and men.
To help, to share,
To grow, to care.

Ignorance
b r e e d s
hatred

Knowledge
i n v i t e s
understanding

Acceptance
f a c i l i t a t e s
harmony.

24

Everyone's yelling
about embracing different
In fellow beings
But true acceptance
is quiet,
beginning with
embracing one's own shade
first.

25

Too often are differences
mistaken for flaws
And conforming
mistaken for perfection.

Assumptions
rooted in prejudice
Discredit encounters
that are potentially special,
maybe even life-altering
Simply because
people are easier
seen as representations
Rather than individuals.

An origin story
is only that,
Not the whole
journey.
Not a life defined.

With everyone so busy claiming
to be misunderstood,
most overlooked the capacity
to understand.

There might be similarities among
insecurities,
Convincing of a common strength.

Do not discriminate
against another's happy.

Too easy is it to misunderstand life's punctuation:
Where a comma might feel like a full stop.
Or the hope that a full stop is just an ellipsis...
Maybe ignore the inverted commas "sometimes"
See exclamation when there isn't any!

Stuck surrounded by symbols signifying
so much more
misinterpretation could be catastrophic;
but get it right, and the story's almost always
poetic.

A broken heart's
out for closure
But a bruised ego's
out for revenge.

Too often
Rose-tinted glasses
Take away the ability to recognise
red flags
With discoloured evidence,
dulling the danger to their wearer.

Leaving a bad situation
for better
is leaving everything.
Besides,
prisoners
aren't expected to visit prison
even if they did
befriend a few guards.

Should something come
to an end,
And future plans vanish,
Refrain from discrediting the past,
And all those memories,
cherished.

35

Regretting anything
that once brought joy
In any measure
Isn't fair
to any moment's happiness.

Forever was claimed
Yet the end prevailed.

The trick
was to cherish everything
before the full stop.

Till another sentence inevitably began.

Search the ruins
for beauty to be kept
And let time ravage
everything else.

The mind will cope,
When the heart accepts it.
The heart will heal,
When the mind allows it.

Hope is strongest
in the silence of nights
igniting dreams.

40

Solitude need only
be given a chance
For its sweetness
to be felt
And its inspiration
to enchant.

Ambience

Aren't we all just flowers, she thought.

Struggling to survive, to thrive.
Different colours, different soil, covering the
world with our existence.
Varied families and origins, but flowers just
the same.

Maybe what separates us
from true flowers is that
they know they gain nothing from wishing
another's petals fall off.
They only blossom themselves,
all turned toward the same sun
shining down on everyone.

In a world where
White is melting
Green is dying
And grey is growing
It's easy to forget
The beauty of nature.
Simple and sweet
Where vibrant colours
Each and every hue
Come together,
Often finished with the sheen
of morning dew.

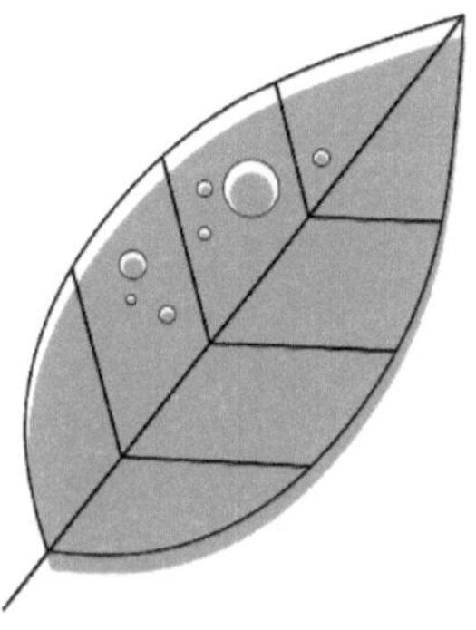

45

A rose's worth isn't measured
by how many people stop and stare.
It is beautiful regardless;
effortlessly, without a care.

Living flowers
are boldly beautiful
But in death,
they turn to experienced
storytellers.

An island,
an untouched paradise
has never once asked
to be discovered,
To be poked and prodded
for the adventure
of others.

48

Treading on soft mulch below
With a canopy of leaves above
Surrounded by earth's aroma,
One can gain respite from
the rat race
of concrete jungles and diplomas.

The steam
billows on its path upward
Only swayed, never extinguished
by nature's jostle
Before again staying true,
till its source runs cold.

The sentiment
behind bouquets
outlives
their mortality.

If she were a butterfly,
She'd use
her two days
to plan a whole life.

52

While the waters
invoked her emotions.
The stars
inspired her thoughts.

She loved watching the sun set into the sea.

The way it gradually, consistently
went down each day,
only to rise again the next morning.
Granted, the ball of fire
wasn't the one even moving
but it was more magical this way.
And she'd hold onto any magic she could.
Specially the kind that
couldn't be captured within pixels.

54

At sunset, pink hues blend
into the sky's blue canvas.
Orange and yellow intersperse
just above the horizon.
If only the mortals would look
and follow that example of
breathtaking harmony.

Even a consistent river,
following a defined path,
enjoys newfound freedom on
meeting an endless ocean.

A light summer breeze
was capable
of offering reprieve,
But a harsh winter wind
could set one straight again.

Sunrise
Punctual, consistent
Waking, greeting, embracing
And always at its very own pace
Saluting, sinking, sleeping,
Quietly, magnificently
Sunset.

The dull bits
though unwanted
Are tasked with
making the colours
Brighter, louder, happier,
The vibrancy of a rainbow
more valuable
against the rain stained sky.

Peace is blue, contentment too;
calm and true.

Where most would consider
clear skies a happy day
She preferred one
shrouded by intermittent
white fluff
A little character
on the vast canvas above.

The winds of change
might threaten to extinguish
fiery passions
But the embers
could sometimes survive
the long haul
to be reignited,
Be it for social justice
or personal relationships.

She liked the rain.
How it lulled
her chaotic mind.
Steady beat and cool winds
gently stirring through the rut.
Precipitation
dousing
the heatwave of stress
that suffocated her into fatigue.
A whole sky
romancing her to relax.

She thought travelling
to be wandering
with purpose,
To wonder about
better than that
which surrounded her.

She wanted to feel the sand under her feet
while walking under the stars.
She wanted to hear the lapping of the waves
without the hustle and bustle on the shore.
She wanted to see the moonlight
mirror perfectly against still waters.
She wanted to take in the seashore
as she never had before.
An experience can change entirely,
after manipulating lighting.

Lying near a babbling brook,
everything illuminated by moonlight,
she wanted to use flames
from her fingertips
to scrawl her thoughts
against the heavens.
Instead of fire across sky,
she settled for pen on paper.

The stars inspire
They do not define.
The stars form constellations
They do not shape lives.

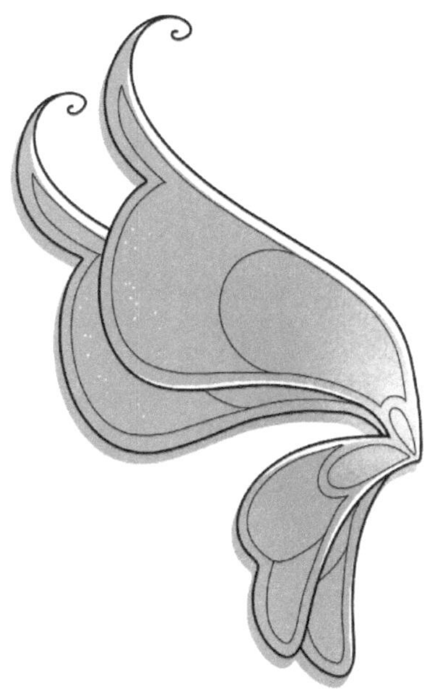

At twilight,
she would expect
fairy tales
to defy their fiction
and come alive
There,
right between
possibility and daylight.

68

Nocturnal silence
pairs beautifully
With beating hearts
and ticking clocks.

She would hang onto
the crescent sliver
in the sky
Waiting for storytellers
to take her hand
and fly.

Reliably, the moon
Reflected back
just enough light
To orchestrate
the majesty of nights.

There is enchantment
in a sunrise,
in a kind word,
in an amused smile,
in a sunset,
in between stars
There is magic
in the world
One need only
revise their definition.

The Land of Shadow and Fog

Knowing her was delightful
But wanting to truly delve
into what made her tick
was frightful,
Shrouded by a one-way mirror
and changed subjects
round every corner
There was method to the madness,
a specificity in every cog
But without
her explicit guidance
it was a land of shadow and fog.

In the corner of her mind
there is a place
Much like a room forgotten
As foggy as a bathroom mirror
With a chair by a window
and a table between them
Its surface used for creation
Mostly on paper, mostly by pen
She'd visit so often for clarity
Brushing her hand across
the blur of her thoughts
Till they could be rearranged
to something better
Something of art.

If poetry were literal
There wouldn't be any romance
in a leaf
Kissing the ground
as its final act
In fall.

The art of fantastical fiction
Lies in giving structure
To illusion.

Should all the books burn
And expression be discouraged,
With all else stripped away,
Language and thought
thereby connection,
will still remain.

For a writer,
Life can be more
Love can be secure
Friendship can be perfect
Death can be honourable
Horror can be contained
Grief can be catalytic
Time can be finite

Reality,
can be orchestrated.

Childhood
is indubitably believing
in immortal balloons
always seeming to stay,
While growing up
is eventually accepting
that they rise like smoke
or wither away
And its finite time
still purposeful,
whether a few hours
or more than a day.

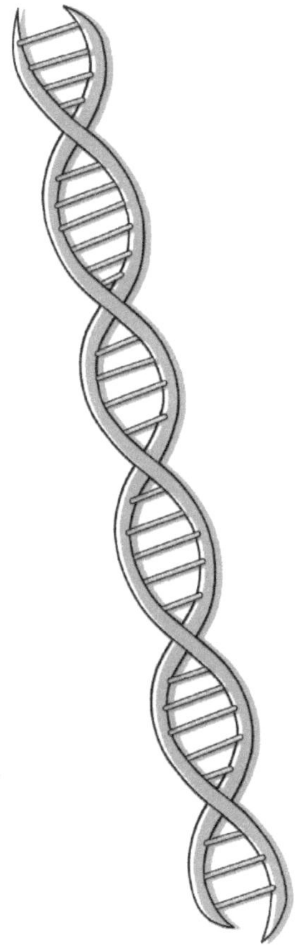

When elements make contact
They combine to create
Or resist to retain
Or alter to accommodate.
They have individual qualities
that may be dominating or dormant
when introduced
to another.
Here, science defines
Their characteristics
Their reactions
Their possibilities
Repeat action brings about
uniform results each time
That's chemistry.
But throw out the guarantees,
the studies, the patterns,
And that's people.

Creativity can be
inspired by mere dust motes
Dancing to exist
in the streaming rays of sunlight
wafting into
a seemingly empty room.

She is a diamond
personified,
created precious
from pressure.
As tough, defined
and clear cut.
But just as the valuable stone,
too much force
could very well break her.

True beauty is uncompromising.
It is quiet, graceful.
Existing peacefully among
the lesser, modern takes
of its species.
Unfettered whether
its presence is recognised.
Because true beauty is superior.
And it is timeless.

Femme

In the beginning
she wanted to rhyme,
Conform to a structure.
But then her musings
needed more room,
to breathe.
So the paper held
an orchestrated mess
of thoughts,
And not a perfectly
proportioned
composition.

She succumbed to breakdowns
under safe privacy
Only to emerge stronger
under inquisitive scrutiny.

Could she crumble
without being labelled dramatic
Could she have an opinion
without being bulldozed for it
Could she refuse
without being tedious
Could she keep to herself
without being conceited
Could she enjoy her own company
without being questioned

They said, maybe one day.
She rolled her eyes,
when classified female.

She is angry, not feisty
Frustrated, not fiery
Acknowledge the articulation
and respect her rage.

Misplaced anger
is as destructive
as misplaced guilt.
While one annihilates
The other suffocates.

While impulsive outbursts
are loud and destructive
She found quiet fury
to be feared and effective.

As the anger ebbed away in time,
indifference and tolerance
disguised as patience
coasted in with the tide.

92

It was fallacy
to worry about
repeating herself
When what she had to say
was worth hearing twice.

None had the right
to question her absence,
after taking the privilege
of her presence for granted.
Because somewhere
in between,
She replaced her insecurity,
With self-worth.

She could be

as captivating as a mermaid

But nevertheless

proved to be

as deadly as a siren.

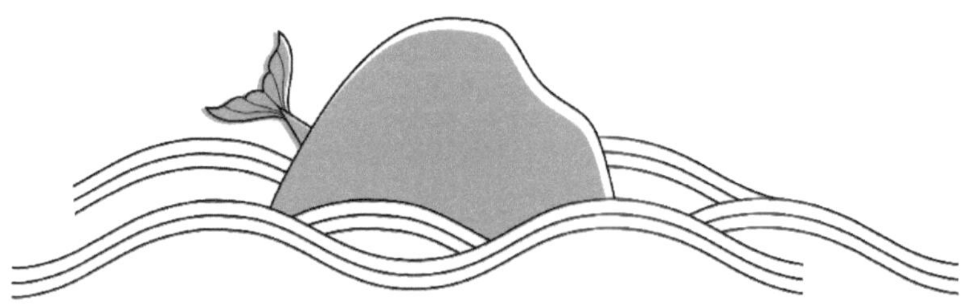

Manipulating psychological assumptions
kept things interesting.

Those charged
with governance
restrain
what they
disagree with,
And flock
to those echoing
in agreement,
Never comprehending
the power of ideas,
Only ever giving in
to their ignorant fears.

There was a halo of diplomacy
in her manner
that equally
baffled and inspired.

98

Being a one-way mirror,
her window never slaked curiosities.

Presumption of innocence
is a fine principle
in essence
Till its loopholes
compel
a vigilante's justice,
At times as calculated
as female fury,
A glitter crusted claw
To the jugular.

She personified a storm,
Magnificent at a distance
And deadly up close.

Life isn't
all that intimidating
If the stilettos
are comfortable.

It must be a woman's
prerogative
to change her mind
if it is a man's
not to use his own.

It often took
retreating into
her mind palace
To return
to a tolerant state.

Why pretend to be a puzzle
Awaiting a missing piece
To be considered complete,
When one can be a portrait
Of life's adventure,
An exquisite, individual
Masterpiece?

Emotions
might be involuntary,
But actions
are pure decision.
Consequences
could be unknown
But reactions
can be controlled.

Instead of
stooping down
to their habitual level
She stepped over them
ever so gracefully.

Mirror dancing
in strutting heels,
styled hair
And sashay for days
is cathartic.

Think twice and again
before crossing
the innocents;
A heart
that was fragile
Grows cold, unfeeling
Their trust and security die
As their skies, once blue
bleed pitch black
in daylight.

Her mistake
was extrapolating him
to the whole population.
And she was still
unravelling
the extent of her flawed outlook
Not enough to abandon it,
rather enough to tweak it.

She had to
remind herself
that nuances in conversation
Don't scream as loud
to everyone else
No matter how much easier
it would be if they did.

Memo to self:
Wonderful words
could be
weaponised
in the warmest
of ways.

She was crystal clear
with her arbitrary
multifaceted
demeanour.

Any side of her could either
shine or blind.

Her first draft
was a raw reflection
of what she felt
And her final edit,
what she permitted them
to see.

She would try,
Then repeat the effort
Once.
But without
satisfying reciprocation
or decent justification,
She'd let them wander
right out of her life,
Back onto the playing field,
appropriate for games.

She weathered trauma
And grew up wise

She survived absence
And fell in love with her presence

She witnessed arguments
And modelled maturity

She feared aggressive behaviour
And strives only for personal peace

She wished for security
And controlled the rest of her life

She lived eccentrically
And given a chance,
wouldn't change a thing.

She refused
to freely give away
what must
rightfully
be earned.

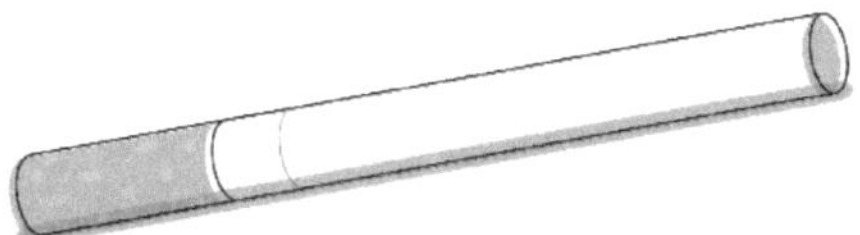

The world might try to
Lead her astray,
But her values would always
Coax her the right way.

Sometimes,
a hug
is as disarming
as a bullet
is lethal.

For ages she had looked
Through people's words,
Always coming close,
but never spot on.

Till the day she was
no longer lost,
Finding all that
she was looking for
in her very own
thoughts.

Perhaps, perchance
One day,
she might dance,
with an air of esteem
that nobody dare question
For it would be foolish
to challenge her predilection.

What a life she led
leaving pieces with so many,
Never enough with one
to ever unravel her mystery.

Living isn't for
the faint of heart.
It takes faith, forgiveness
hope and love,
Beginning toward
oneself
before the rest.

A princess needn't
belong to a prince
to be queen.
Royalty runs
through her veins,
She need only tap into it.

124

And plainly put,
she was worth her expectations.

Serendipity

Conversation
was the way to her heart
She admitted it without hesitation
Hidden in jest,
Only clear
to those that noticed
the quiet twinkle
in her unassuming eye.

Whenever she could,
she'd lend a listening ear
a shoulder to cry on
a humorous remark
a decent time
But only when it wasn't
at her own expense.
Some understood
while others faded away.
But she never lost sleep
at the end of the day.

They were her home,
the people in her life.
Creating memories that warmed her
from the inside out.
They are her home.
Ever evolving,
Ever loving, ever laughing.
Occupying heart space
for ever more.
And should she ever have to
renovate or move,
Well, she was resilient enough
to do that too.

Laughter
that she could
smile back on
Was their greatest gift,
one that kept giving.

She chose
to bookmark her bliss
And return
to the scene of the smile
whenever she so pleased.

Being comfortable
is being open to shatter
like delicate glass,
Maybe they'll cherish it
Maybe they'll lose their grip.

Acknowledging
the failings
in someone's nature
Instead of
justifying them
Can avoid
lasting heartache.

134

Confusing comparative
for superlative
is an invitation for agony.

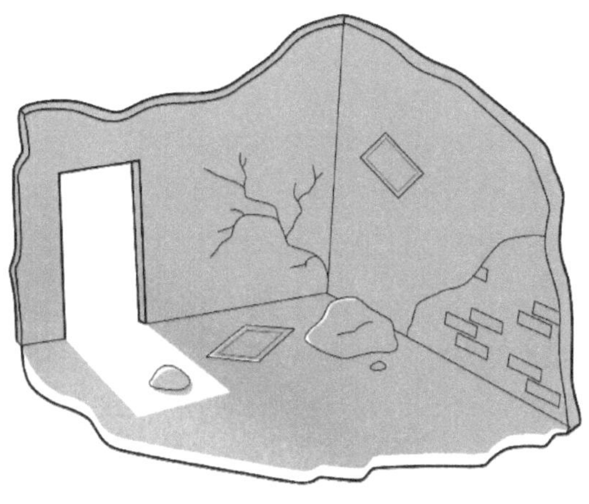

It might take disaster
to level structures
of shelter,
But a breath of betrayal
can easily demolish
figurative ones.

Just as stars shot
across the night sky,
As momentary streaks of light,
She'd had perfect exchanges
with faceless strangers
Before they too faded away,
out of sight.
And though none lasted
all that long,
Each one had its magic
before inevitably moving along.

So to all those who coaxed
a happy sigh,
Thanks for stopping by.

Stumbling upon a connection
is pure happenstance
Coaxing it further
is decisive commitment
Letting it fade or sever
is conscious neglect.

Embrace the loves present in life.
Don't miss out while waiting
for a quixotic one to come round.

What is a soulmate
but a distorted
yet tangible
reflection of oneself
In studio lighting.

Soft skies
Knowing winds
A park bench
And of course,
his playlist
Took her to Paris,
just like that.
Her imagination
And his soundtrack.

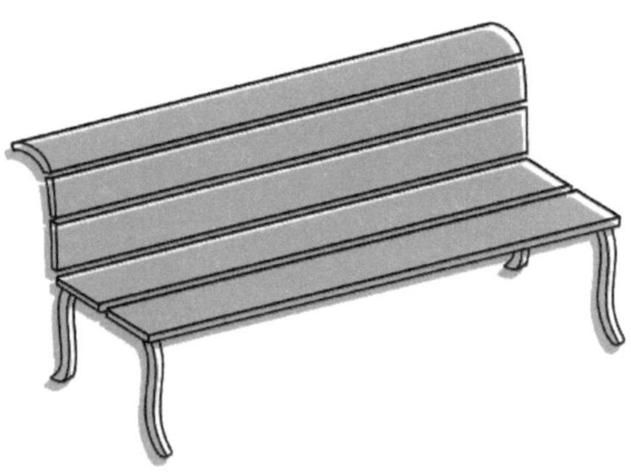

Perhaps
yearning for romance
in every corner
of every interaction,
Turns a blind eye
to potentially
beautiful relationships.
If love's the destination,
the scenery along the way
offers quite a view.

She favoured that space;
between nothing and something.
It was her favourite phase.
The former being strangers
and the latter
being unspoken pressure,
the middle was the sweet spot.
A silhouette,
the endearing outline that let her fill in
whatever her heart desired.

In a garden of many,
One has the choice
between those with thorns
or those with none,
Classic, inside and out
- beauty
Or run-of-the-mill ordinary,
- pretty.
Between those worth it,
And those who are easy.

She was brilliant,
no doubt
But one tends to forget
last night's star
when something brighter
comes around.

Should one find another
that fills their days
with the magic of night,
embrace the calm,
bask in the glow
But do not forget
daybreak is at dawn's door.

146

A bond
that forms overnight,
Might not fit quite right
in broad daylight.

The contradiction,
consequence and calamity
of feelings
Might best be summed up
By the notions of
falling in love
and growing to hate.

No relationship
is a bed of roses
But,
it shouldn't be
a coffin of nails either.

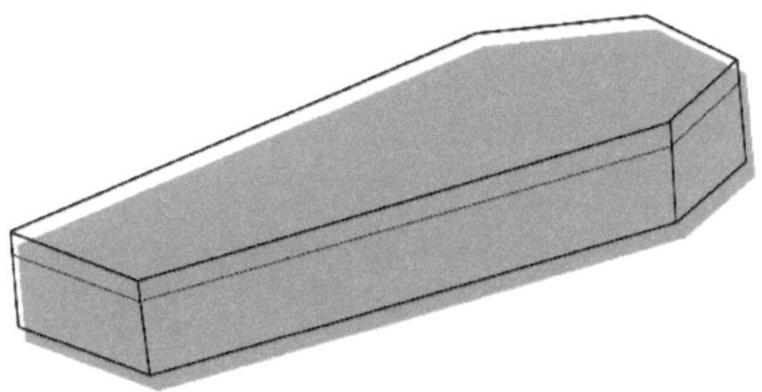

Maybe minds attract
Souls comfort
And hearts,
pay the price.

The real risk
of living
and by extension
of loving,
Is the simple
yet precarious balance
of expectation
and settling.

There is nothing
easier and more romantic
Yet harder and more frightening
Than choosing one person
over and over again
For love is nothing,
if not a continuous decision.

Vicariously,
her heart discovered
that no daytime declaration
could ever be
as loud
as pure truth
whispered
under the night sky,
fingers intertwined.

Making her laugh
was no difficult task
She had quite
the sense of humour
But making her smile
was a distinct feat
All its own to savour.

Ancillary Anchor -
He stood steady
Surrounded by chaos
Unmoved by uncertainty
Still, amidst volatile waves
Waiting patiently
For her.

The picture of security
She dreamed of
But never let herself expect
Surrounded by chaos
For her,
He stood steady.

He watched her twinkle
to her own rhythm
Content to ride
her winding trains of thought,
Attentive,
candidly appreciating
the scenic route to her point.

She'd meet him in her reverie,
immaculately free.

157

Her manner was enchanting
to those that valued
Content over packaging.

She wanted to be magic.
Not the kind
that put on a show
But one whose presence
lingered
long after
she'd passed through,
She wanted to leave behind
subtle specks
of her light
Not as to overpower
But just enough
to make a quiet difference,
to dispel
some of the weighted darkness.

Falling in love
is so often mistaken
for committing to love
That she couldn't
take either
seriously.

She knew of romantic love,
The who, how, why
But she wouldn't ever trust it
in real life
She couldn't rely on something
so volatile,
arbitrary,
flawed,
Something so very human.

She preferred
to fantasise silently,
from afar
To avoid
being hurt violently
up close.

No baby blues
or emerald jewels
Would lure her
into compromising
the witty spark
Behind her soulful
iridescents.

What a strange thing
to look for love
elsewhere
when one doesn't
feel it within.
For it's hardly something
that can be lost and found.
Rather, something that
is recognised, nurtured
And if it's fated,
reciprocated.

Rather than search
for a missing puzzle piece
to fill a phantom void,
She focused on growth instead.
Completing oneself
is far more rewarding
Than gambling
on the game
of fairy tale loving.

Her heart
was on the horizon
And chasing either,
Proved
a fruitless endeavour.

In a myriad of voices,
She befriended her thoughts.
In a trend-setting period,
She discovered her different.
In a co-dependent era,
She embraced her solitude.

Inventory

She was made up of verse,
Beneath her prose armoured skin.

Her playlists
could spill secrets
But her varied taste
created a labyrinth
of a library
that locked them away.

She was as deep as the ocean;
as pure as the blue sky.
The world couldn't be trusted
So she lived a colourless lie.

172

She was easy, yet difficult
Warm, yet stone cold
Accessible, yet aloof
Once appropriately put:
She was a fancy contradiction;
And owned it.

She didn't want
haute cuisine
experimentation
thrilling adventures
And blackout fun

She wanted
lazy mornings
cafe afternoons
balcony evenings
And rooftop nights.

174

She used to wait.
Wait for better
Wait for the future,
Wait to explore
Wait to be found.

Then one night,
She began to write;
About things she wanted,
Of being contented.
Acknowledging her role
As rightful protagonist,
She authored her awaited bliss.

What one chooses to do with time,
Speaks to where priorities lie.
And not keeping any for oneself,
Amounts to a pitiful crime.

Having grasped that concept,
She began making an effort
Carving out time for herself,
An exercise in self-worth.

The sound of silence
was one she
Often yearned for
Seldom experienced
And always appreciated.

A blank canvas
is a catalyst of inspiration,
unearthing emotions.
Calming the chaos of her mind.
In stillness, like an ocean's.

178

She wasn't nearly as fragile
as she felt sometimes,
It was pleasantly endearing
to realise it now and then.

She preferred
a contented hum
To thrilling percussion,
A consistent melody
Rather than
erratic beat drops.

There isn't
a spontaneous speck
about her
Including the subconscious.

She wouldn't stand out
in a crowd
But once encountered,
it was hard
to remember a time
Before the gift
of her presence.

Her inner resplendence
outshined her average veneer,
A secret earned
only by her chosen few.

She had a curious mind
An empath's heart
An unconventional spirit
And self-evident principles,
bolstered
by quiet confidence
That made peer pressure
quake.

184

It was near impossible
to mine her
for anything substantial
And just like precious stone,
what lay beneath
the surface
Was tantalising, rare
and difficult to uncover.

The fiscal failures
around her
unconsciously nurtured
a second-hand
once bitten, twice shy
approach,
Forging pecuniary responsibility.

At first
she wanted money
To try to buy happiness
But later realised
she wanted security
To maintain safety,
comfort and contentment.

Light shed on her eyes,
they sparkled
And when shed on her wit,
simply irresistible.

She treasured
unwrapped trinkets
and unexpected kind words
so much more than
timely gifts on annual occasions.

Her reckless decisions
were a mighty rare occurrence.
But those exceptions
almost always involved
starting a novel,
At midnight.

She was an open book
in a world that didn't care
for punctuation.

A philosopher's head
With a poet's heart
And level-headed impulse,
She need only
Her own company
And a chance
For her thoughts
To come out and dance.

She could go
Days
without speaking a word
Weeks
without seeing anyone
Months
without human touch
But not a waking moment
without twirling her thoughts.

Try as she might to explain,
befriending oneself
Seemed a hoax to most;
Though to her
it was the dream,
For when everyone
receded
With circumstance or time
She still had herself
To keep company
at no wasted effort or dime.

Her ability
to accurately
articulate herself
was admired.
With alliteration,
always
the amusing apple
on top.

She forged a new melody,
instead of living in the echo of his wrongs.

She fought a war within her
between passion and practicality;
Some days
her heart poured out on paper.
Other days
her head planned for the future.

Happiness is.
Present tense.
Past is reminiscing about it.
Future would be yearning for it.
But in between is the sweet spot.
The coveted fuzzy feeling.

That's what she'd do;
Manipulate happy to present tense.

She wasn't fashionably late, she was punctual.
She wasn't spontaneous, she was meticulous.
She wasn't easy-going, she was responsible.
She wasn't exuberant, she was forbearing.
She wasn't quixotic, she was perspicuous.
She wasn't exciting, she was dependable.
She wasn't flirtatious, she was witty.
She wasn't fun, she was funny.

The personal ad writes itself, doesn't it?
She didn't think so either.

She wasn't meant for another,
And she lived happily ever after.

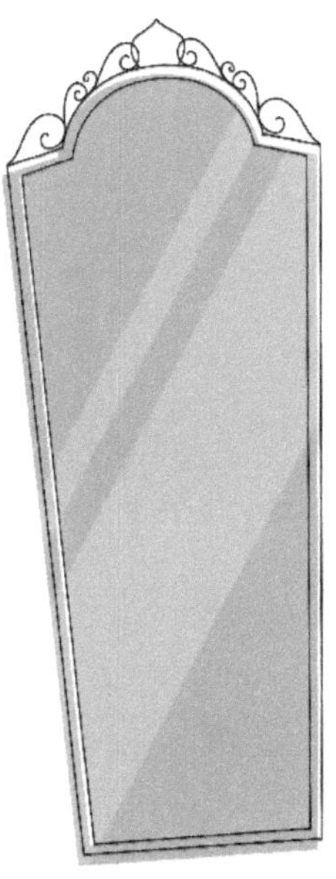

Most scoured
all over
Looking for The One
Fortunately,
hers was in the mirror
Competition? None.

With no roadmap restrictions,
the world was her oyster
Both with its pressure
and its potential
For that pearly future.

Solitary was her default setting.
Her resting heartbeat.

A love that lacks commitment,
is a love wasted.
Thus, she committed to herself.

She was obscure enough
to seem intriguing
But diplomatic enough
to keep them guessing.

She mimicked her eyes.
Unassuming, average every other time,
But breathtaking
in just the right light.

What a pity it is
To doubt one's informed judgement
For a second opinion.
To forfeit worthy self-perception
For external validation.

She didn't mean to brag
But humility
came easily to her
Almost
every single time.

At rest, she was lounge jazz
without the cigarettes.

And when she was gone,
In her words
they'd find her living on.
Timeless thoughts
penned down
The muse, her reflection
plus the crown.

About Anna

If she wasn't scribbling in her notebook at a café downtown, Anna Belmonte was planning her next breath. Working in finance, she dotted her i's and crossed her t's during office hours and then some. But on her own time, she dared to put pen to paper with only coffee and contemplation keeping her company.

INKFEATHERS PUBLISHING

India's Most Author Friendly Publishing House

Stay updated about the latest books, anthologies, events, exclusive offers, contests, product giveaways and other things that we do to support authors.

 Inkfeathers Publishing

 @InkfeathersPublishing

 @_Inkfeathers

 @Inkfeathers

 Inkfeathers.com

We'd love to connect with you!